From Five to Fifty

How to Lean in to Your Entrepreneurial Spirit

Reneé Marie Smith, Esq.

ISBN: 978-1-4834-9012-0 (sc)
ISBN: 978-1-4834-9011-3 (e)

Library of Congress Control Number: 2018909883

Because of the dynamic nature of the Internet, any web addresses or links contained in this book may have changed since publication and may no longer be valid. The views expressed in this work are solely those of the author and do not necessarily reflect the views of the publisher, and the publisher hereby disclaims any responsibility for them.

Any people depicted in stock imagery provided by Getty Images are models, and such images are being used for illustrative purposes only. Certain stock imagery © Getty Images.

Lulu Publishing Services rev. date: 8/27/2018

For My Dad, a man who inspired and encouraged
a shy girl to conquer the world

We must not cease from exploration and the end of all our exploring will be to arrive where we started and to know the place for the first time.

T.S. Eliot

Contents

Introduction

Throughout my life, I have continually relied on a basic set of business tools or business mind-sets to help me.

I call them tools because I'm remind of a mental tool-box. Household tool-boxes contain a few valuable tools (hammers, screwdrivers, wrenches) that are simple in form. Ones uses them to perform manual tasks that show up in our daily lives. No cords or electricity needed.

Simple manual tools are limited because they address only the most basic needs, such as hanging a picture, assembling a bike, or tightening a leaky faucet. However, fulfilling those basic needs can transform a house into a home.

My basic business mind-set tool box holds a collection of mind-sets that I learned while growing up. My dad is an entrepreneur who used stories to build an entrepreneurial mind-set in me.

These business mind-sets instilled me with the confidence to try new things, take chances and experience extraordinary things.

This book shares these business mind-sets because rarely does a business meeting, client conference or friendly chat pass that I don't recall one of my dad's stories to help illustrate a point.

Seemingly complex issues can be resolved by using simple mind-sets that build success.

Plan Beyond the Goal

It's how you deal with failure that determines how you achieve success.

David Feherty

I grew up in a suburb of Cleveland in a development of similar houses filled with children. I was a shy three-year-old child but that didn't stop me from having a best friend, Linda. Her backyard abutted our back yard.

I was at Linda's house one afternoon playing Barbie's when the urge to use the bathroom arose. Being shy I didn't want to tell Linda or ask her Mom to use the toilet so without a well thought out plan on time and distance, I choose to run home to use my training toilet seat.

To a three-year-old this was great distance, also running is never a good idea in this circumstance. My goal was just making it through the front door as from there my mom would help me.

I rounded the front of the house with time to spare. I was relieved when I arrived at the front door with dry pants and tired legs only to discover the door was locked. I knocked and rang the bell patiently waiting for my Mom. The door swung open, Mom was there and just then my will gave out. There on the front stoop of my house I learned a valuable lesson from my wet pants, reaching the bathroom should have been the goal. Sometimes need to plan beyond the initial goal to account for unknown circumstances. This evolved into an interesting business mind-set.

Start with a goal in mind and then plan through it to a different end point to account for unknown factors. If a new project fails, make sure to review the goal and was it properly placed.

If the result was not achieved chances are the goal was misplaced. Whether the anticipated result was money, public relations, brand awareness or a combination of several factors making sure you work through even the point of your proposed end is important.

Ventures will have unexpected events that change the course of the project. These course changes require resources to adapt to the new path or return to the original path. Using additional or unexpected resources will affect what your goal should look like and when it will occur. Setting a goal and time frame that is past the original ending point of achievement will increase economic efficiency of resources, maintain momentum and increase the likelihood the goal is better conceived pivot point which can be used for the next project.

Leave behind and take away: Forget fixed plans. Keep outcomes flexible and plan past initial ideal goal concept to adjust for unexpected factors.

Business Mind-Set #2

Teamwork Pays

Talent wins games, but teamwork and intelligence win championship.

Michael Jordan

When I was five years old, my family went to Disney World. Walking around on my little legs limited what I could see and experience. It was crowded. I was getting sandwiched between bigger people. I could only see everyone's kneecaps and rear-ends. Not the excitement of the typical Walt Disney experience. I quickly realized that my vantage point would be much better if my dad carried me. "Daddy up," and it became my phase of the day. Once in my dad's arms, the Disney World experience became much more exciting.

Years later my dad told me that my chirping, "Daddy up? Daddy up?" though exhausting at the time, made him smile when he thought about that trip. He was patience and helped me because he understood that the view from his arms was far better than the view from my own legs. Both my dad and I had a richer experience at Disney World that day because of the team effort. A new business mind-set was added to my toolbox.

Nothing in life is achieved without other people. The term "self-made" is often used to describe a successful person but that person has not succeeded on their own. They have had to surround themselves with a support network to achieve. Employees, clients, and friends are a vital key to business and career success. Without them, no business can operate or be profitable.

A year after starting my law firm I was struggling to keep up with the work, but I was too frugal to hire help. A trusted client stopped by my office unexpectedly and saw me in a harried state. She smiled, said "It's time for you to hire a person to help you." I was reminded of my dad at Disney World. It was so much more enjoyable when I was able to see with his help. My client suggested that if I wanted to achieve a higher success level with less stress, I would need more hands, and she was right.

After I hired my first employee, my business productivity increased exponentially. She added forty hours a week to the effort behind the business. Clerical work that held me back due to lack of time or energy was redistributed.

My efforts refocused on increasing the incoming client work growing the business. Plus, it was more enjoyable to have someone to work with on projects and support to work through problems. I went from working alone on my laptop in my kitchen to a six-person office, an office computer network and five subcontractors.

One of the most important, yet difficult, decisions in business is deciding when to hire and expand. To increase your business' output, you need the help of others. Teamwork can increase productivity. Done correctly, hiring staff, subcontractors or temporary help will make your business more well-rounded and exponentially grow.

Leave behind and take away: Talent or smarts won't sustain success. Entrepreneurship is a team sport. The view is better because others support you above the crowd.

Business Mind-Set #3

Informed Choices

Miracles happen every day, change your perception of
what a miracle is and you'll see them all around you.

Jon Bon Jovi

One Sunday afternoon my dad was watching golf on television. I sat down for a few minutes to join him, but at age seven it didn't take long for me to become bored. I made the over-generalization that golf was boring and asked why anyone would sit and watch it. With quiet disapproval my dad replied, "Watching golf is boring to you because you don't understand how challenging the sport is and you haven't taken the time to appreciate the skill it takes to play it."

I left the room wondering how golf could be anything but boring and what it would take to change my perception. This process added another business mind-set to my toolbox of wisdom.

Many of us judge and qualify the events that happen in the world around us. We do this automatically as we sift through our daily tasks. Often, we quickly draw conclusions about people or circumstances from limited information or appreciation of the truth. A linear point of view determines our choices, which results in only seeing one straight path forward. We fail to notice the many events occurring at the same time. Life is not linear; it constantly twists and turns, full of different people, perspectives and its multidimensional.

I frequently share Stephen Covey's story from The 7 Habits of Highly

Effective People. He writes about how a perception, or mind-set shift, with information creates knowledge to see the truth in the situation, thus allowing you to make a good choice.

He relates a visual example of a father with two young children. As they board a subway train, the children are running around and disturbing other passengers. The father sits without any care for his children's actions.

A man sitting next to him turns and says, "You should really mind your children." The father lifts his head, looks, and says, "I know I should do something, but we are just coming from the hospital where their mother died. We are all struggling with that news."

Our perspective changes from the beginning to the end of that story. First, we have the information about the train environment, the noise and the children misbehaving. However, with the knowledge of the family's loss, we are better able to choose a knowledgeable response based on multidimensional information. We often apply information to everyday situations and make decisions only to find out later that we didn't have the best vantage points.

Over the years, I changed my perspective on golf applying the same mind-set. I have tried over the years to learn this sport. Taking golf lessons and tried my friends' patience while I struggled on the course. My opinion has not changed that golf is boring to me and golf didn't become a passion of mine, but it takes great skill to compete at the level of the athletes on television. This opinion is now based on real understanding of the game.

Ignoring the opportunity to gain at least one additional viewpoint prior to making a generalization about a situation that will impact your business is a mistake. Avoid making choices from a linear perspective based solely on your experiences. Find a viewpoint from a customer, competitor or an unaffected third party to give a more rounded perspective. Create a mind-set that searches first for alternate perspectives to see issues or events multidimensionally.

Information is a stream of unorganized data. Knowledge is information that has been organized through multiple perspectives combined with situational truths that create solutions. Then solution making mind-set creates a basis for a good business.

Leave behind and take away: Stop generalizing. Limited viewpoints result in limited life, career or business results. It's perspective. An investment in multidimensional knowledge creates a perspective for good solutions.

Business Mind-Set #4

Keep your Behavior Consistent

She trusts people who are trustworthy. She also trusts
people who aren't trustworthy. This is true trust.

Tao te Ching

When I was ten-years-old my dad seemed concerned about something. I would ride with my dad when picking up building supplies for his construction sites. My dad is a builder.

Riding with him was great because there were so many people constantly in our house, five kids plus friends, rarely did one have an opportunity to be with him alone. He is a great story teller, but this day he was unusually quiet.

Several hours passed with little conversation when he looked over at me and said matter-of-factly, "This morning, I watched a friend treat another person very badly." His eyes went back to the road. I sat silently, waiting for him to continue and the silence lasted for two more stops to pick up supplies.

When he began again he said "I was confused by his action as in that same hour my friend was kind to another person. So, I asked him why he treated people differently. He surprised me when he said it was because the second man had been kind to him. Confused I asked why he treated the first person so poorly. In which he responded, 'Well he treated me poorly.'"

"Reneé, treat everyone with kindness because you are kind. Be a good person always, regardless of how you are treated. Consistently on who you are, not one way or another based on how you are treated."

I listened to what he said but being ten years of age, my interactions were limited to playground rules and birthday party politics. However, the many experiences I have had since that car ride have shown me how vital this business mind-set was for my toolbox of wisdom.

When I first began writing, and subsequently learning how to promote my books, I met many people who were more experienced in these areas. I relied whole-heartedly on many people's advice and some of the trust was misplaced. Several of these people had also provided services to other of my friends with unsatisfactory results. Rumors that these people were untrustworthy and suggested not having any contact.

Remembering my dad's advice, I was determined to remain who I was at heart, treat them kindly and leave the door open these individuals to make right the situation when the opportunity presents itself. Both individuals ultimately made good on their promises.

You can't separate life mind-sets from business mind-sets. Who you are in private will be who you are in your career/business as well. I understand that people don't always come back to correct a misstep, but I consistently work with the mind-set that I am honorable, regardless of another's be-havior. To operate your business by treating different clients or customers based on how they treat your or your staff will result in a cloudy brand vision and poor customer service.

Simply design a motto for your business and apply it consistently to all customers and vendors. Over time this consistency of message will be rewarded.

Steven Covey says, "You can't talk yourself out of something you behave yourself into." The reverse is also pleasantly true. Honest behavior builds trust with the intended person and with others who witness that behavior.

Leave behind and take away: You can't control the actions or motives of others. Make choices based on your own core values and operate your business with a consistent brand message.

Business Mind-Set #5

Value Judgments

Patience doesn't mean making a pact with the devil of denial
ignoring our emotions and aspirations. It means being
wholeheartedly engaged in the process that's unfolding,
rather than ripping open a budding flower or demanding a
caterpillar hurry up and get that chrysalis stage over with.

Sharon Salzburg

G rowing up my room was packed full of stuff that was overflowing out of drawers, closets, and boxes. I felt that every "thing" had a value and was useful. There was no need to throw it out. Well, after one too many requests from my mom to clean my room, I lamented my dilemma to my dad.

He was honestly sympatric to my dilemma and went on to explain how one large company dealt with this issue, The Caterpillar Corporation is a major industrial manufacturer.

Every few years they inventory the spare parts warehouse and throw out spare parts even though they are worth thousands of dollars. It becomes more expensive to store, maintain, and insure them over time then the part itself is worth. This equation diminishes their present value. Once again, I added this business mind-set to my toolbox.

Energy, time, employees, and other components comprise a thriving business and life beyond money. Innovation is key to keeping a business thriving. One must develop a methodology for determining when something with value needs to be removed to make room for something better.

Everything and everyone in a company has value. Also, current trends and other innovation are vital to attracting new opportunities. An example is equating the present value of a new computer system that will be outdated in a certain number of years but increases productivity today. Another example is hiring and training a temporary person to fill a vacancy that may become obsolete instead of hiring staff person to learn the company culture and transition to new role once the current need is eliminated.

I apply this multidimensional value calculation in all areas of my life. I use it to determine the best use of my time, other people's time, and long-term investments. In business school they use the term—present value or future value. Today, I simply call it my Caterpillar value. What choice will be the best use of my resources?

One should instinctively analyze spending resources to preserve a status quo and their ongoing cost. Do you find yourself spending hours or money on errors or situations that cost you more in the end?

Remember to apply the Caterpillar value. Learn that letting go, moving forward, and making space for new opportunities will often save you money, effort, and frustration. It will also help you continue your momentum forward by integrating new ideas with available energy and resources instead of trying to store and protect what has a lessor value.

Leave behind and take away: The price tag does not always determine value. Create a system to determine value from a multidimensional mindset based on cost which considers resources used, efforts directed, and other opportunities not utilized instead.

The Bank Bag Theory of Organizational Structure

Honesty is the first chapter in the book of wisdom.

Thomas Jefferson

When I was in eighth grade, my dad bought a twenty- table pizza restaurant. It was a traditional restaurant set up with the red and white checkered table cloths, long and narrow, with booths on one side and standalone tables with chairs in the middle.

My dad was running his construction company, but he thought it would be a good idea for my brother, a sophomore in high school, and myself an eighth grader, to understand what running a business was like. I took the bus there after school and on weekends to work. Every night, the day's receipts would be totaled, zipped in a canvas bank bag and secured with a lock. Then money filled bag was deposited in the bank's night depository.

During a morning bank bag pick up with my dad I asked, "Why the heavy lock on a canvas bag? All a person has to do is take that bag or cut the canvas to take out the money?"

Dad replied, "The bag is designed to keep those people who are honest from stealing. The goal of the heavy lock is to remove the temptation from the person who wants to be honest. See I've learned that a small number of people who intend to steal and will when the chance arises. There is very little you can do to prevent this type of person from theft because stealing is their intent.

"However, most people are honest and won't steal. They want to work hard and do their best and if you have a system like these bank bags, that make stealing an obvious act by cutting the bag or taking the bag, they won't steal. Sometimes you won't be able to tell the two types of people apart, but that isn't important. It is important that our business methods deter the first group and don't tempt the second group at all. That is what these simple bank bags do." This business mind-set ended up in my toolbox of wisdom.

Some people say, "Trust no one" and so these businesses reflect this oppressive attitude. I disagree. This lesson from my dad built on the idea that people will choose to be honest and it's the entrepreneur's job to design an environment that removes temptations and promotes team skills.

My endeavors have thrived because I have incorporated the "bank bag theory" into all my relationships. Instead of rules and regulations that suffocate creativity in favor of security, I give the people that I work with the latitude to succeed.

Applying loose guidelines that remove or limit methods that could easily be corrupted for personal gain. Also make sure there are opportunities for personal advancement for those wanting to succeed within the organization. If people are rewarded for extra effort or results within the business, it reduces the need to create ways to subvert the system for personal gain.

People accept jobs to succeed and not to fail. If they do fail, I hold the organization responsible. The bank bag theory when correctly applied will ensure the majority of employees succeed.

As a leader, the responsibility is yours. Businesses grow when there is opportunity and people are rewarded for jobs well done.

Leave behind and take away: Don't worry about dividing people into trustworthy and untrustworthy categories. Create business environments that promote personal success within the organization.

Business Mind-Set #7

Always easier to improve your lifestyle

Build a lifestyle around your brand, and the audience will follow.

Eva Chen

I have been earning money since I was twelve years old and I have been running my own business since I was thirteen. Frequently I had extra spending money. As my reserves grew, so did my habit of impulse buying. Little thought was given to limiting this habit since my business kept providing an income.

I left for college and my cleaning business clients replaced my services. My cash flow dramatically decreased. I had not counted on having to find all new clients or a job after my freshman year.

Mentioning this downside to being self-employed with my dad he simply said. "A cat gets stuck in a tree because it's harder to come down than go up. Same thing with lifestyle. It's easier to adjust when your lifestyle is improving and it's much more difficult to adjust when you need to downsize your lifestyle because of reduced cash flow. Identify a base line lifestyle below your current income level. Learn to save the rest. When your cash flow decreases you can supplement it with saved cash to maintain that lifestyle instead of changing your lifestyle every time your cash flow changes. This way your day to day lifestyle does not swing from high to low with income levels, and it reduces your stress because you know you always have a predetermine lifestyle." And so, a new business mind-set.

This is an important concept especially to entrepreneurs as cash flow is important when running a business that needs to provide for both your personal finances and the business. If you starve the business by reallocating cash so you can have an expensive pair car or pair of shoes you may lose or delay a business opportunity. Alternatively, you cannot deny yourself a basic lifestyle and think that it won't affect your enthusiasm for the business. The business must provide the fuel for your personal life engine whether that is monetarily or inspirationally. Suffering in your personal life for the life of the business will result in frustration. You need to experience the joys of entrepreneurship or end up surrendering the business when things get lean.

The business is a vehicle for you to achieve your life goals and every vehicle needs fuel. Make sure you have a backup savings that stores fuel for your business to avoid having to choose between business opportunities and your personal lifestyle.

Leave behind and take away: Forget budgets. Define a baseline lifestyle that your business can support and save the rest of the income regularly, so you don't have to choose between yourself and your business.

Business Mind-Set #8

Misdirected Energy

Idleness is to the human mind like rust to iron.

Ezra Cornell

Dad was the walking suggestion box in our house. He would filter our grievances about how things were or were not going. However, the grumbling of my siblings was met with firm statement from my dad, "You have too much time on your hands if you are just complaining. Get a job and then you won't have time to complain." The discussion was over. An important business mind-set was added.

So, complain once, complain twice and then fix it. Complaining is not a business plan, but a sign that you are wasting energy, time and ignoring the possibilities of growth which will result in problem resolution.

Resolve the problem through action. People rely on complaining as a substitute for long term problem resolution which requires a decision followed by action. Complaining may be a good way to vent frustration but should be a one-time event where you list what is wrong then go about a way to fix it.

Time is a resource. Energy is a resource. Neither should be expended on complaining which is not a solution-based action plan. Worse yet, complaining can also be a crutch for one to look to others to solve their problems.

In business the issues we face often seem outside of our control and we tend to blame other people or other things. For example, the suppliers aren't cooperating, the market is bad, or the clients no longer want the products. Notice when these excuses become the scapegoat for not revising your business model.

Businesses are living, breathing entities. They are not static enterprises. Many times, the issues that seem to prevent our growth become the innovation necessary to move our business to the next level if we apply our time to creating a solution.

I catch myself when I circle around a problem too many times without taking steps to analyze, correct, revise, or remove it. A realization that my faultfinding has become an excuse for inaction.

The complaining plan to resolve problems just transfers one's control and input over the situation to an unknown outcome, likely to result in more complaining and waste of resources. This cycle of inaction can be seen in many businesses. Feel free to vent and then go solve the problem. Your job is to reveal problems then find solutions to the issues in an objective space or time. This can often result in hidden opportunities.

Got complaints? Take the time used to complain and get to work fixing the problem.

Leave behind and take away: Complaining is not a success strategy. Use excess energy to create solutions.

Business Mind-Set #9

Success is Expectations Met

*Opportunity is missed by most people because it
is dressed in overalls and looks like work.*

Thomas Edison

At twelve years old a business started me as an opportunity fell in my lap. Which often happens with opportunities. They find you and all you need to do is say, "Yes."

A friend of my mom's asked if I would clean her house for thirty-five dollars. I said "okay" and so it began. My business grew by word of mouth. Over time I realized the pay was better than the hourly jobs available to me at the time. I didn't lose my Friday and Saturday nights to babysitting children. Cleaning houses was a better option.

My friends didn't appreciate my new business. They thought it was gross to clean other people's dirty houses. My dad typically didn't comment about my work. When he asked how things were going I shared my friend's comments about my business being gross and demeaning. With a smile, he said, "Did you achieve your goals?" I said, "Yes." "Then they are wrong." He walked away.

Sometimes it's that simple with another person's advice on your business or career. It is just wrong or doesn't fit the facts. Added another business mind-set to my toolbox of wisdom.

Objectively this business was a vehicle to achieve my two personal job objectives: maximum dollar per hour and more free time. I had time and earned more money than traditional jobs for a twelve-year-old. I set my own schedule, plus got paid on the spot, most the time cash.

Like every job, some aspects weren't pleasant, but my goal for my business to be successful was met. More money and fewer hours. Simple.

The job or business you have today should help you achieve the immediate result you desire and put you on a path towards a long-term goal. Fulfilling that requirement will produce the success you want. The product or service you offer may not be to everyone's taste but that should not matter to you. The result is the point.

I have seen many businesses fail or be abandoned because the owner or team felt it wasn't producing an ego result. Let your business and/or career make you money and then use that money for your ego. Not the other way around.

A lot of times money is made by businesses or jobs that other people don't want to do or work at. That is why they are called opportunity and some aspects of opportunity aren't always sexy.

Leave behind and take away: Drop judgements. Dirty jobs and unglamorous businesses can be profitable if you see them as they are, a means to your goals.

Business Mind-Set #10

Everything has a System

A bad system will beat a good person every time.

W. Edwards Deming

My high school home cleaning business had organizational systems. These systems were not intentional. The systems developed organically out of addressing business needs. I stumbled into the business mind-set that everything is subject to a system. Learn the system so it can be utilized and improved.

First system addressed amount of time per house. I charged a flat fee per house to determine my hourly earnings. The earning rate helped me assess whether this job was more profitable use of my time versus other jobs. Increasing how efficiently a house was cleaned and decreasing the time needed to clean directly impacted my profits.

So, I outlined a plan of work the first time cleaning a house. Starting at the furthest point from the front door cleaning my way to the front door. Avoiding entering a cleaned area once complete. Each time the home was cleaned by using the same plan, the cleaning routine became faster and the system for that home got more efficient. This increased my hourly earnings on that home.

Second system developed as the business expanded with more houses to clean. This issue meant more travel time and different customer schedules to work around. Increased travel time meant less time to clean and higher overhead, as more gas per day and wear and tear on the car.

A multi-house system was designed by scheduling certain houses certain days based on location and amount of work for the properties. The time needed to clean each house decreased due to system one's efficiency and travel time between houses was streamlined due to system two. With the scope of work remaining static, profit margins increased for each house.

Another benefit was with my strategically planned cleaning schedule, more houses were completed in a week because of less time per house with less driving. The multi house system increased the number of houses able to be cleaned in a week. The profits skyrocketed.

The increased profits meant funds for increased customer service. So, if a customer had her home cleaned two or more times a month, she would get a ten percent discount for each cleaning. This meant more revenue and less work each time because fewer days between cleanings meant the house remained cleaner. The time needed to clean was reduced even more. I then could fit more houses to be cleaned in a day.

Happy customers use your service more loyally and frequently refer friends. Referrals poured in and was earning $750 a week during the summer or $3000 a month in 1985. Looking back its pretty amazing since I was 16 years old when my business took off. This home cleaning business provided enough income for me to pay cash for my first year of college.

Every business model can have a system designed for it to maximize business' success with efficiency and increase customer service.

Systems are a necessity of growth. They form either organically to resolve business growth issues to create more capacity for growth or to reduce cost. Conversely outdated or poorly implemented systems can stunt growth. The key here is to notice the issues and then design a system to address it.

Even in a career setting, understanding how the systems of your company work will enable to you better utilize them for your advancement and success or improve on them to highlight your skill set.

Leave behind and take away: Don't let present tasks distract you from developing organizational systems. Understand what issue may restrict achieving a desired business goal and design a system to overcome it.

Business Mind-Set #11

Performance Mind-set

I fear not the man who has practiced 10,000 kicks once, but
I fear the man who has practiced one kick 10,000 times.

Bruce Lee

My dad and I were watching the 1984 Olympics and Mary Lou Retton were competing on the balance beam. Her performance seemed effortless and graceful. Mary Lou was my age and I wondered what I could achieve with such effortlessness. I mentioned this to my dad, and he said, "Yes she makes her routine look easy, but do you think it is easy to tumble and jump on a four-inch-wide beam? A gymnast's goal is to make her routine look effortless because it's the effortless nature that makes something so difficult, beautiful. However, to achieve that effortless beauty she had to practice that same routine over and over, for minutes and hours, then days and years whether she felt like it or not until it was second nature for her body and mind to achieve it. Dedication creates the appearance of ease."

Making very difficult achievements look effortless became one of my core business mind-sets. Practice results in achievements but dedication to achievement is what makes amazing feats look easy.

Your business should look effortless through practice. People go to work every day, but few make success look effortless. Success in business is not achieved by aimlessly going through the motions of a job or business. Don't confuse making skilled work appear effortless with easy tasks.

Business success is based on well-developed skills or habits and developing these skills requires a training program much like a gymnast.

The secret lies in what Mary Lou Retton achieved. She started with basic gymnastic exercises. Once that exercise was mastered through repeated practice, she could build a routine of exercises. Then with a routine learned she could add in difficult elements like speed or dance steps. She consistently repeated the choreographed routine until it was an instinctive habit. Now when she was called upon to perform the routine it was delivered effortlessly because it was a learned skill or habit.

One attains effortless business success by identifying success building mind-sets. Consistently applying them to develop good decision-making skills then consistently using these skills until they become instinctive or a habit.

Dedication to developing successful business decision making skills requires resilience. It is years of intentional planning and dedication. This unnoticed effort required to consistently face and overcome business obstacles is done without accolades. This is the muscle building that's needed so when it's time to perform, the instinctive application of skill or habit appears effortless, like a gymnast.

It is these business instincts that make business success possible.

Leave behind and take away: Success isn't a lottery. Consistent daily efforts to achieve your objectives lead to habits of success.

Business Mind-Set #12

Everyone Is Needed

So, whether you're a gem in the royal court or a stone
on the common path, if you accept your part with
humility the glory of the universe will be yours.

Tao Te Ching by Jonathan Star

When I was fifteen, my dad took me to McDonald's for lunch. I love their French fries. I commented on what a hot job it was to work the fryer and I wouldn't want to do it. He said, "I like having someone to fix my car, and I like having my groceries checked out at the store. Remember, Reneé, the people who do these jobs are important to us because without them our daily lives would be more difficult. Treat everyone with respect, regardless of how you see their job, they are important to your life."

I thought about my dad's advice and how many people I relied on every day to do their jobs so that my business life progressed or was made easier. I realized that I had taken them for granted and decided immediately to treat everyone who assisted me with gratitude whether it was a simple "Thank you sir" or "After you ma'am." Surprisingly, with that mind-set, I found my life became easier and happier. I realized how much help I received from others every day that had gone unnoticed. I added another business mind-set to my toolbox of life.

Have you ever stopped to think what your life would be like without sales clerks, and garbage collectors? They make our world go around, even if we prefer not to do those jobs ourselves, they are no less important.

Salary, prestige, or acclaim as you define them may not be what others value.

This business mind-set should be in the forefront of your career or business. Once I paid attention to how many people it took for me to complete a project, no matter how minor the role, I understood more clearly the term team effort. Value every person who makes your business or career successful.

Successful businesses are defined by their cultures. Cultures value each part. Cultures create systems that evolve based on perceptions and most of the time, the perception of people's value starts with the person on top. Value every person who makes your business or career successful.

Leave behind and take away: You can't invent a wheel without spokes. Every person is valuable and the job they do is valuable to you. Be respectful of everyone.

Business Mind-Set #13

Money Is a Tool

Money is only a tool. It will take you wherever you
wish, but it will not replace you as the driver.

Ayn Rand

There are five children in my family and with seven people to think about, the budget was always a consideration. However, the budget never came before an experience in our house. All of us children participated in extracurricular activities, sports, summer camps, musical instruments, drama club and horseback riding. All of these had a price tag attached times five.

As my dad was dropping me off at a volleyball camp when I was fifteen, he shared a conversation he'd with one of his friends. This gentleman suggested my dad to stop encouraging us children to do so many activities. "It will save you money, Mike," he explained. My dad told me it is not how he saw life. "I want you to learn Reneé, money is just a tool. Not the end." He explained the work starts with me, but he would help me with the financial tools I needed to begin the process of becoming an interesting person in pursuit of an interesting life.

A new business mind-set was born, and it became a lifetime passion. An unerring desire to be interesting and to live an interesting life. I invested in learning about food, wine, art, travel and music. Educating myself. Through this process I meet like-minded people what are on their own explorations to make their lives interesting.

Life is a series of experiences, some free and some that have a price, but the ability to explore new experience develops curiosity for the unknown.

An openness to interesting experiences is the foundation of entrepreneurship. Being inquisitive about new experiences helps one recognize an opportunity when presented and the learned trait of saying "yes" opens avenues to success.

Use money for long-term planning to make your business open to new opportunities as well. Find investments (tangible or not) that will create future expansions that may not be apparent at the present. Create a culture of curiosity of the new and unknown to keep your business innovative and alive.

For example, spending money on brand building. Apply this mind-set. Invest in an image that your company is interested in innovation and new ideas. Open to client development and concerns. Willing to expend funds to remain informed. This requires investing in intangible experiences for your staff and clients.

Avoid the trap that money alone creates interest. Money for money's sake will attract initial attention but it's fleeting. Like passing flashing lights on the highway. Your eyes are drawn to the strobes but you only thing about the circumstance momentarily.

Brands and businesses are like people, what is interesting attracts more interest. Maintaining interest means it must be interesting. Being interesting requires an investment.

Leave behind and take away: Money does not create. Money is a by-product of creation. Money invested in the product or person for creating an interesting experience will attract and hold attention.

Business Mind-Set #14

Know a Little about Everything

Wisdom is the daughter of experience.

Leonardo da Vinci

My first car was a diesel Volkswagen Rabbit. I bought it for $400 when I was sixteen. It felt great to buy it with my own money. It was like crossing a threshold towards adulthood.

However, I didn't understand that $400 cars require constant tender, loving care to keep running. One day, I wanted to meet my friends out, but the oil indicator light came on. With a diesel engine that meant real engine problems if not addressed prior to driving further.

My dad suggested changing the oil instead of just adding more oil. I had never changed a car's oil before. As a reflex, I asked my dad to do it. He agreed, but he only had time the following day, which meant I could not meet my friends that evening.

I thought to myself, "How hard can it be?" Dad talked me through the steps. Since it sounded straightforward and I can follow directions, so I began. I did not deviate from the instructions, but my dad had assumed I was smart enough not to have my face under the exact spot where I pulled out the plug to drain the oil.

When I pulled out the plug to drain the oil I had limited mobility. I turned my face just enough, so the dirty engine oil hit my hair. The oil was gross and sticky, but I finished the job, slid out from under the car and proceeded to get ready for a night out with my friends.

I was pleased that I had overcome the engine light issue and was on time for my friends that night even if it meant I had a black streak in my blond hair. It became another business mind-set.

Be willing to learn various jobs, seek new information and if need be lend a hand to keep your business moving forward. I have an expansive reading list and constantly scan magazines and news outlet to hear about new ideas to promote and increase business. This awareness and desire to learn about unknown areas is vital to be a managing entrepreneur.

In life and businesses my motto is find a way. Many times, that means learning about whatever aspect of the business needs attention and managing the issue. The broader your information base is on finances, organization, mechanics and personnel the better positioned you are to make good choices.

Starting the business is just the beginning of the work. Maintaining and growing a business requires diversity of knowledge, openness to being out in front and learning new techniques. Trying these new techniques is the breath that keeps the company alive.

Leave behind and take away: Never stop learning. Ideas aren't formed in a vacuum. A willingness to learn is a vital trait in entrepreneurship.

Business Mind-Set #15

Identify Systemic Problems

Some guy hit my fender, and I told him, 'Be fruitful
and multiply, but not in those words.

Woody Allen

F ive kids, all with different activities, made getting a driver's license and
buying a car at sixteen a necessity. The freedom of being able to walk
out the front door without waiting on Mom or dad and go where I wanted
to go was an awesome idea.

I had been working since I was twelve and I had enough savings to buy
a car. It did not need to be an impressive one, but it had to start, move and
get me where I needed to go.

I registered at Sears for my driver's education as soon as my birthday
was within sight. I was thrilled to receive my shiny new license on the first
test try. To me the driver's license certified my driving accomplishment
but a ticket and a few minor dents later, I should have re-examined this
assumption.

Returning home one evening from a hair appointment, I saw debris
blown onto the road of the car I was following. As a new driver I didn't
understand this as a warning sign and to be alert.

The driver slammed on their breaks to avoid it. Bam! I ran right into
the back of the car. Bam! The car behind me rear-ended my car. It was a
car crash sandwich.

It was no minor scape. Both the front and back bumpers of my

Volkswagen Rabbit were smashed in an unbecoming way and there was no way to hide it from my dad.

After the required police visit and another traffic ticket, I returned home with my wounded car and my wounded pride.

I relied on the fact that my older brother and sister also had driving mishaps before me. I figured my accident was just another "kid" event. My dad didn't see it that way. He sat me down to have a discussion.

He came right to the point and said, "This is not just a dented fender; this is a sign that we have ignored your lack of driving skills when other some minor mishaps occurred and with this major accident, we need to address this problem now. Your six-month driving record tells me that you are either reckless, distracted or both when driving and I need to work with you before you get seriously hurt. Not just the fenders on the car."

One traffic ticket or accident warned of an issue with my driving. Both of these events, which already happened, demonstrated that my skills were un-tested, and more care was needed when driving. But multiple accidents and each time getting more severe is a warning sign that can't be ignored. An important business mind-set was learned.

Dad taught how to understand the road hazard signals and what driving errors caused accidents. I couldn't wait to learn how to drive. But my over-zealousness to be able to drive myself ignored what real driving is about. Driving safely to your destination.

Running a successful business requires the same awareness. Spot problems when minor but continue to reoccur. An employee who is continually late, reoccurring shortage in supplies or computer systems that keep shutting down. These minor issues are symptoms of other issues to come that could negatively impact your business like a computer crash losing all the business's data.

Applying the mind-set that minor reoccurring issues need to be addressed in order to prevent disaster. Stop and take the time to resolve the underlying problem. Avoid waiting until there is a major problem that damages your business.

Leave behind and take away: Don't let enthusiasm distract you from reoccurring nuisances. Symptoms point to areas that need correction. Fixing minor issues prevents major problems.

Business Mind-Set #16

Never Skimp

Quality, service, cleanliness, and value.

Cavett Robert

While I was growing up, we owned a station wagon. It was a necessity in our family since there were a lot of people and things to cart around. Over time, the station wagon became cluttered and dirty from all the human traffic going in and out.

One day, when my dad was driving me home from school, he looked frustrated. Earlier in the day, he had given a teacher a ride home. He had felt embarrassed about the all the clutter in the car, and now he was concerned. I think he made up this statement on the spot, but it has stuck with me and become another important business mind-set: "No matter what our economics are, we can be clean and keep our things clean. Remember that effort is free."

Having a low budget doesn't mean that your business isn't successful or that you are less likely to succeed. Quality isn't a price tag or a label. Service isn't always delivered on a silver tray, and value can sometimes come from a blue-light special.

It is important to find a base level. Don't use a lack of funds as an excuse. Businesses do it all the time. They say, "We don't have the resources now," "Our people aren't as trained as other companies," or "We can't afford that location."

Step back and look at how many success ventures started in a garage.

Microsoft, Tupperware, and Mary Kay all worked on the premise that economical limitations can be overcome with enthusiasm.

The effort to maintain a base level of care (care for the company, care for your clients, care for the image you portray) doesn't have to come with a hefty price tag. Most of the time, it just takes effort.

Starting out in my firm, I was the accounting department, the head of human resources, in charge of inventory control, and so on. Anyone who has started or managed a business understands how to wear several hats at once. At times, my laziness—or just plain weariness—would cause me to skimp on the presentation.

One day, at an on-site presentation, a trusted real estate agent stopped me afterward and said, "Maybe, in the future, it would be nice to give your clients a personalized folder for their paperwork."

It was as though she had shot fireworks or banged a drum. She was right. I had never overspent my budget, and her words did not offend me. I knew it was her way of saying that, no matter what my economic situation was, my clients were important and should be reminded of that as often as possible—if even just with a simple gesture.

By the time I did my next presentation, I had delivered. After the meeting was over, I gave my clients a smart folder with my business card and company name embossed on it. Proudly.

Life gets busy, and our internal energy becomes low. Always remember that you have the base level and treat customers as important—no matter what the budget.

Leave behind and take away: Laziness undoes a polished image. Not lack of funding does not. Customer service need not be sacrificed due to economics. It's is often free, and it is vital to say thank you with every transaction.

Business Mind-Set #17

Start from the End

Your business vision is sacred to success. Remember a vision is not always clearly defined; it is like an oasis in a desert. The caravan knows to follow the path on faith, even if sand obscures it.

Louis V. Gerstner Jr., *Who Says an Elephant Can't Dance?*

I wanted to play volleyball during my first year in college. I received the information about tryouts three months before the tryout schedule and began working on the physical requirements, specifically running five miles a day. It seemed daunting, but I would start every day. At first, I was only able to run for ten minutes. Then, it was thirty minutes. Eventually, I was running five miles in the morning—and five more in the evening. During my runs, I would visualize myself playing volleyball: returning a spike, setting the ball, and serving. I ran for hours, and I focused on achieving the moves.

I arrived at college and began the tryouts. Running with a group and over hills was much more challenging than running by myself, but I did it competitively. Going through the drills and the moves I had visualized seemed hard but mechanical. I was optimistic that I would make the team.

After several weeks of tryouts, the roster was announced. I did not make it. The coach told me that she admired my attitude and enthusiasm, but she didn't have a place for me. I was defeated and stopped playing.

Several months later, a first-year student who had made the team stopped me and said, "You know, if you had asked to practice with the team, Coach would have let you. You would have improved your skills—and maybe you could have made the team next year."

This life-altering lesson became a business mind-set that I decided I would never forget. I didn't start from the end in my thinking. If I had, I would have realized that goals are not always achieved on the first try. Don't stop. Find another way.

Let's look again at my conversation with the coach. "Reneé, I don't have a place for you in our lineup this year, but I like your positive attitude."

"Thanks, Coach. May I keep working out with the team? I want to keep working on my skills."

"Reneé, that is a good idea. We always need additional players to scrimmage against."

I could have asked a player who was selected for suggestions to improve my skills. Maybe she would have asked the coach if I could work out with the team. I don't know if I would have made the team the following year, but I do know I would have grown as a player.

I lost an opportunity, but I promised myself I would not repeat that mistake. I transferred to a new university and played volleyball the following year. I even ended up playing against the team and the coach I had tried out for the year before. I am glad they could see that I didn't stop, and I am glad that I played volleyball in college, but it wasn't the same. I only played for one year.

Achieving your goals doesn't just require going through the physical motions and visualizing your success. It requires walking down the road to that success—even with all the twists and turns or disappointments at first try.

Leave behind and take away: Don't want to get lost in the process of running a business. Where do you want this experience to end and start planning from there.

Business Mind-Set #18

Sift the Wheat from the Chaff

Everyone who wills can hear the inner voice. It is within everyone.

Mahatma Gandhi

For my second year of college, I chose a university that was scholastically more challenging than where I started. This academic opportunity also came with a much higher price tag. The tuition was four times as high. Some of my family members expressed displeasure in my choice, and that resulted in months of no contact.

I decided to talk with my dad about my decision and the reaction of the family members who would not speak to me if I transferred.

He said, "Everyone is motivated by his or her own experiences, current life, daily events, and desires. This doesn't mean that they don't love you, that they want to you to fail, or that their advice isn't the best they can give. However, only you can decide if their opinions or advice are right for you. Develop the ability to hear your inner voice and choose which path is right for you. I made a mistake when I was younger. When a person I didn't like gave me advice, I automatically did the opposite. After many years, I learned that this method of choosing a path—based on my opinion of the person giving the advice instead of the advice itself—was wrong. Though I didn't like the person, I realized that much of his advice was shared with the best of intentions. His life experiences gave his opinions a different vantage point that I should not have automatically disregarded. Developing the ability to think objectively about people's opinions, circumstances, and emotions—in even the most subjective matters, like picking a school—will become one of your most valued assets."

I had a new business mind-set.

My life's trajectory was changed in a positive way. Attending the new university propelled me into a new level of self-confidence. I was more secure in my decision, and I better understood myself in the process.

This result reinforced the mind-set that balancing others' advice against your inner voice is good. This mind-set develops faith in making decisions because the decisions are their own creations—not just accepting another person's perspective. The success or failure is owned in a positive way.

One of the most thriving industries in the United States is giving business advice. Opinions, books, and seminars abound when one sets out to open a business, start a new career, or try something different. That is often a positive thing. Seeking information to create multidimensional knowledge is important.

However, one should look at this mind-set of how to integrate an outsider's advice in a business situation and not just apply it. Certain variables that only you know can make their advice inapplicable. These guides are assistants; they are not the boss. You are the boss, and you need to weigh their input against your specific scenario.

Decide what filters are being used when you take another person's opinion into your world. I always take other people's perspectives at face value. After I analyze what they say and the facts they share, I ask myself, "Would that result in a solution to my problem and create the opportunity I need to advance my career/business—or is this just well-meaning advice that is not a solution?"

The idea is to be proactive based on your knowledge, intuition, and skills. No matter what your skill level, if it is your business or career, you know it the most intimately. Don't be reactive to external forces, events, or people.

We learn how to accumulate advice and sift it through a mind-set of success that is based on the business mind-sets expressed in this book. When you believe in the result wholeheartedly and apply it with passion, your success is all but guaranteed—no matter what your desired outcome may be.

Leave behind and take away: Don't default in another's recommendations. Everyone is motivated by their own desires and intentions. Make your own choices and seek insight from others.

Business Mind-Set #19

Value Is Multidimensional

Life is a series of experiences, each one of which makes us bigger,
even though sometimes it is hard to realize this. For the world was
built to develop character, and we must learn that the setbacks
and grieves which we endure help us in our marching onward.

Henry Ford

I bought my first car when I turned sixteen. The selection process always
leaned toward function over comfort and cost over luxury. I always
bought the basic four-wheel-transportation type of vehicle to get me from
point A to point B. When I graduated from college in 1990, a new car
was my reward. The time had come for me to drive a car that screamed,
"This woman has made it!" At least, I had made it out of my undergraduate
studies.

In contradiction to my previous car purchases, I decided to buy the
most luxurious and expensive sports car I could afford. This twenty-year-
old's bravado only lasted until I realized the price of new car and understood that monthly payments would be required. The payments seemed
like the financial equivalent to Mount Everest.

I was nervous and apprehensive about the monthly obligations since
I was still nailing down a job and wanted an apartment. The $300 per
month seemed daunting, considering the frugal college budget I was used
to living on. Hundreds of dollars every month for five years was a scary
proposition.

I turned to my dad for advice, and he went back to the dealership with me. I showed him the sports car I wanted—and the cost associated with it—and we talked about my decision.

I said, "How do I commit to making these payments, Dad? Maybe I should rethink this idea."

My dad doesn't give advice directly. He felt that part of growing up is learning to weigh one's decisions and learning how the process unfolds. Instead of giving traditional advice, he would share stories and let me decide my path. He felt learning from an objective standpoint removed the emotions that could hinder or skew a decision. We talked about the sports car as we drove home.

He said, "As your father, I should tell you to buy a beat-up old taxicab. You're just out of school, and you should save money, play it safe, and plan for your future. This reminds me of a friend who loved Corvettes. As a teenager, he saved pictures, researched, and dreamed of the day he would own one. He waited his whole life, yet it never seemed reasonable or logical to buy one. Finally, on his fiftieth birthday, he went and paid cash for the Corvette of his dreams. He told me how he drove that new beautiful car out of the showroom and onto the highway. As he headed home, he savored every moment of the experience he had waited thirty-four years for.

"Pulling into the driveway, he got out of the car, looked at the one thing he had always wanted, and went inside. We talked the next day, and he shared something very insightful. He said, 'It was fun to drive, but it would have been more fun when I was sixteen. Even if it hadn't been brand-new and needed repairs, or hadn't been completely paid for, I missed the experience of a young man enjoying a sports car. I know now that I should have done it then.' He sounded so sad."

And that was it. Dad said nothing further about the payments being too high or too long. He didn't mention being too young or waiting to see if the job worked out. He ended the story and walked into the house, leaving me with another business mind-set for how to determine the value of things on a multidimensional level.

I bought the car, and I loved that car. I installed two new transmissions in it since I had so much fun shifting gears. All the cars I bought between age sixteen and twenty played an important role in building an executive decision-making process, but that one brought me joy. I valued the experience of being a twenty-year-old with an awesome car.

Many factors determine a successful business or career trajectory. Deciding how to facilitate your best path comes down to determining the cost of buying something, signing up for something, or hiring someone. Value isn't always one-dimensional and monetary.

Looking back, I'm not sure if the gentleman and the Corvette really existed, but my dad's story had a big impact on me. I learned how important it is to look at the big picture in life. People say, "Life is a journey," but in my mind, it is also a series of experiences that create a continuous story to be viewed over the years as we progress and grow.

The same goes for your business and how it appears to the outside. Money is a tool to not only buy or acquire things but to create a mind-set and image. That is why people suggest dressing for the career position you want instead of the one you currently possess.

That doesn't mean you should buy something illogical by saying it would be better now than later. Instead, ask yourself where you want to go, where you want to take your business, and who or what you want to become. Compare your daily choices with the vision of the life you desire.

For example, do you take a job to learn the skills that will put you on the path to your long-term career goal or take a job with a bigger paycheck today.

Same is true for a business. Taking on a new customer, opening a new business line, or investing in infrastructure may be the best use of your resources—even if they cost more at first.

Leave behind and take away: A dollar is not always just a dollar. Value decisions should be made with a long-sighted approach. Look at the monetary, time, or energy investment today in terms of a long-term strategy of where the company, its employees, or even you should be.

Business Mind-Set #20

Timing Is Everything

Open the next office before you are ready.

Barbara Corcoran, *Use What You've Got*

As a results-oriented, type A person, I wanted to complete my studies and get a job. I love lists, and I wanted to check off the education box.

A mentor gave me some good advice as I was approaching the end of my undergraduate studies. She said, "Wait, work, and then go back full-time to the advanced education you know you will need. By rushing into what you think you want without the benefit of working first you won't have all the facts. You may select the wrong path because your decision is about what you think you need instead of knowing what you actually want since you lack the real-life experience of what it takes to get there. Work in the field you think you want to see if you still want that education after you have some practical knowledge. Then go back to school full-time instead of working and going at night. You will enjoy school more."

This advice goes in the top five pieces of advice I have ever received. I started at IBM, and I didn't like it. The corporate world was too rigid for me, and the structure didn't lend itself to advancement. I bounced around for another year or so until I fell in love with the law. I didn't fall in love with being a lawyer in name; I fell in love with how lawyers think. Once I realized that was my path instead of my original plan of an MBA, I quit my job and went back to full-time law school.

I relaxed and enjoyed the process of law school since I already knew I could support myself. I had work experience, and I felt no anxiety. If law school didn't work out, I wouldn't be in dire financial straits.

Waiting did three important things: I didn't waste years and money on an MBA that I didn't need, I knew I could financially support myself, and I saw the importance of timing. This business mind-set was for my toolbox of wisdom.

It's not just what you do but when you do it that makes it important. When evaluating the costs of a business or career decision, include the present value of the experience and how it affects where you want to end up. Sometimes that means wait. You won't appreciate the experience, education or your business is not ready for that innovation, yet.

When you don't know where to go, what to decide, or how to resolve an issue, wait and investigate. Look at businesses that model your goals. See what steps they took. Use that information to find a path that will provide you with information that will assist in your process. Waiting removes the pressure of having to decide now. Very rarely does one need to make a career or business choice without the opportunity to evaluate it. Time can be slowed down if you learn how to hold the moment and allow the circumstances around you to provide the answers.

Leave behind and take away: Don't be impatient. Wait until you have the necessary information to make a choice. Gaining practical knowledge increases the odds of correctly timing your career and business decisions.

Business Mind-Set #21

Break the Mold

Utility is when you have one telephone, luxury is when you have two, opulence is when you have three—and paradise is when you have none.

Doug Larson

O n the advice of a respected mentor, I worked for several years before starting full-time law school at age twenty-four. I was shocked at how my attitude differed from the other first-year law students.

I no longer saw grades as the high bar for earning a living. I had already successfully supported myself without a law degree. I didn't equate long hours with success. Using hours effectively results in success. At IBM, I realized that the hours I invested there were not effectively improving my skills for other opportunities.

When you follow the same path as others, it is difficult to achieve something different and—more importantly—unique.

I didn't follow the traditional course of starting law school directly after graduating from college. That encouraged me to break the mold in how I approached my post–law school career and subsequent business.

Legal success could be found without joining a big firm with long hours, business suits, and office politics. I am not saying that those things are not right for others. I just didn't value the same type of legal career, and my subsequent success made my perspective different.

After working for various firms for ten years, I started my own firm. I wanted to be an "approachable" lawyer whose clients felt comfortable at my kitchen table. I wanted to be like a family friend who could solve their most personal issues—for a fair price.

I didn't want marble floors, an impersonal receptionist, or an intimidating atmosphere. I believed in my heart that there were people in my community who didn't need those trappings to hire me. I wanted to show how I could make a difference by building a successful law practice in humble surroundings—with friendly staff and no business suits.

Not representing myself like other law firms was not a negative thing for my business. It was positive. My clients saw and felt the difference the minute they walked into my office. Individuality and offering a genuine product will always trump being like the other guys. This concept was a huge success.

Leave behind and take away: Don't be afraid to avoid conventional paths. Conformity often eclipses innovation.

Business Mind-Set #22

Changing Perspective on Fear

Why, sometimes I've believed as many as six
impossible things before breakfast.

Lewis Carroll, *Alice in Wonderland*

As I small child, I fell off a dock while on summer holiday at a lake with my family. I don't know how long I was under the water—I don't think it was long—but I remember the fear of looking up at the blue sky from under the cold water and feeling helpless.

This helpless feeling clouded my desire to be in water. I avoided putting my head underwater at any cost for many years without understanding why.

When I was twenty-two, a friend asked me to join her in getting certified for scuba diving. The image of falling helplessly deeper under the surface flashed through my mind, fear touched me, and I understood why I avoided fun water activities.

Faced with a choice of not joining my friend in learning how to scuba dive, which could be fun, or trying it and overcoming my fear, I took the latter. I would try it and work through the fear.

My decision was made easier when my friend explained that the initial schooling was in a pool with an instructor. Since I felt somewhat safe in the controlled environment, I agreed. By the time the instructor told me that an open quarry dive was required for the certification test, I was already four weeks into the course. Moving forward was the only option because I was enjoying the experience.

Driving to the exam site felt like to driving the final mile to a criminal sentencing. I kept talking to myself about how it was fine, I was safe, and I would not turn around. The hour-long drive was filled with an inner battle between a childhood experience and an adult desire.

Overwhelming emotions on both sides of fear warred within me. When I was thirty feet under the surface, I needed to remove my mask and the breathing regulator. I had to choose how I would utilize my fear. The girl before me was so afraid of the task that she got out of the quarry and abandoned the test. That did not help my resolve.

I held my breath, closed my eyes, and tried to focus on the task at hand, which included not drowning.

I focused on my moments—one at a time. The cold water kissed my face as I removed my mask and breathing regulator. My training kicked in. *Hold mask and regulator and count to three*, I thought. *Now slide the mask back over my head, secure it, and slowly insert the regulator into my mouth.* I could hear the water in my ears, but otherwise, there was dead silence. I opened my eyes when I replaced the mask, and I watched the water draining out as I replaced it with air from my nose.

The underwater world revealed itself to me again, but this time, I was a victor. Exhilarated, I spent the next hour enjoying my success and exploring that underwater world.

The sunlight, the fingers reaching toward me from beyond the surface, and the cool sensation of the water surrounding my body gave me whole new perspective of the day I fell from the dock.

I never used the scuba certification, but I keep the card to remind me of the huge deposit I made that day by trusting myself.

Fear is human and necessary, but perspective on that fear will define you. That experience reinforced my belief in myself. Changing your perspective on fear is empowering, and I added another business mind-set to my toolbox.

I have used this story many times with my clients. Being an entrepreneur means going where there is no path and finding opportunities where others didn't see them.

As a human being, you can't travel into unknown areas without encountering fear. It is instinctive and necessary but harnessing the energy of that fear is vital to being successful as an entrepreneur.

Don't see fear as a red stop sign. Moving into the unknown should feel like a friend standing next to you with his hand on your shoulder. You should feel security in knowing that you are on high alert. All your systems are active, and you are aware of your environment. Your original nature evolves when you go into the wildness.

This heightened awareness makes you clearheaded, more apt to see miscalculations or mistakes that could be avoided and offers insights into correcting errors already made.

I am concerned when I am making a big decision and don't feel fear. That tells me I am not committed to the idea or haven't fully investigated its importance.

The other part of fear is when it comes after a failure. Fear arises from the unknown and from avoiding the same result on a similar path. Embrace this. Think of it as your prehistoric self-venturing into the jungle and being surprised by a bear because you were unaware. On your next trip, you would have your instincts in full awareness so that the bear would not surprise you again.

Fear correctly harnessed is the best motivation. If you have not failed, then you haven't truly pushed your boundaries. Entrepreneurs, by their very definition, will fail at achieving the desired goals time and again. They must—or they won't find the perfect result that brings them rewards.

Fear must be your partner in this process. It will guide your steps to avoid taking the path that resulted in failure. If insanity is doing the same thing over and over, expecting different results, then fear prevents it from happening.

Leave behind and take away: Stop fearing fear. Recognize where a fear is stopping you, embrace it, and find a way to change your perspective on it. Fear is necessary to becoming a successful entrepreneur.

New Kind of Math

Diversity: the art of thinking independently together.

Malcolm Forbes

I grew up in Cleveland, Ohio. One of the most beautiful times of the year is fall. I remember happy times picking pumpkins at farm stands and driving through rolling hills lined with trees sharing blazing colors of orange, red, and yellow as they prepared for winter.

I also remember dealing with the fall leaves as they filled the lawn and gutters. My dad and I were discussing cleaning out the gutters to avoid issues when the snow melted and had nowhere to drain. I said, "No big deal. Bring the ladder. I will start here at the porch and work my way around."

My older brother, hearing this conversation, voiced his opinion that my plan was doomed to fail because we didn't know if the ladder was tall enough. Once I left the porch area, what would I do? He said, "Make sure you have everything you need before you begin."

My dad agreed. So, the gutters stayed clogged. Without any progress or results that day, I returned home. A new business mind-set was placed in my toolbox.

Ever since seventh grade, I knew I wanted to be a lawyer. My older brother is an engineer. This family conference to address a problem shows the difference.

I see the world as a puzzle that needs to be solved. I tell clients all the time that attorneys are problem solvers. We have a strategy, but we assume that facts will arise that we will need to adjust. In our world, one plus one does not always equal two, because equations in the legal world are not direct. With great lawyers, one plus one can equal five—if you have the facts and law positioned correctly.

This is an important mind-set if you are an attorney. If you look at the world as a rigid system and try to eliminate all the variables, you will never begin the client's case because the variables are limitless. Every legal question holds different facts, people, and areas of law. Law is a practice of interpretations. I prioritize beginning, and I adjust as needed to achieve my goal.

Engineering is an exact science, and engineers value precision. They eliminate all known variables before beginning. If you are building a bridge, being resistant to the laws of physics may cause your client problems. No one wants an engineer "interpreting" the laws of physics. Clients want the engineer to follow the laws of physics. Gravity cannot be defeated. It must be addressed. For my brother, having a plan mapped out in its entirety was more important than handling the clogged gutters.

Had I thought it through further, I would have offered to just clean the areas I could reach so there was less work to do later. That way, my brother and I both would have achieved our goals. He would know what parts of the gutters could not be reached by the ladder in the garage, and he would have had less work to do later. I would have gotten some of the gutters cleaned and felt like the job would get done even without me. If I had started it, there would have been less work for the next person.

Understanding another person's math will help you find ways to communicate with each other. Do not take this to mean that lawyers are creative, and engineers are not. It means that lawyers and engineers approach creativity from the perspective of their training and how they have trained their minds to view facts and information. Each profession has its own way of communicating. People are trained to evaluate problems in ways that are consistent with the needs of their jobs.

Leave behind and take away: Entrepreneurial math isn't what they taught in grade school. Learn how the people you are working with evaluate problem-solving, so you know how to communicate with them.

Business Mind-Set #24

Saving Money Is
Wasting Your Time

Empty pockets never held anyone back. Only empty
heads and empty hearts can do that.

Norman Vincent Peale

A t thirty-three, I was caught up in the excitement of real estate. My
dad was a developer, and we grew up around dirt and drawings. We
learned that real estate was a good investment if handled correctly. I was
five years into a new law job in Miami, and I decided—with my extra
cash and good credit score—to renovate and flip houses to make extra
money. I started by buying a one-bedroom, one-bathroom, as one friend
described, "dump" in South Beach. A developer had converted an apartment building to condominiums and was selling the unsold units "as is."
The condominium was in rough shape and needed a complete remodel to
be habitable.

My dad recommended that I learn basic repair skills to save money on
the remodels. *Okay,* I thought. *How hard could it be?*

When I attempted to install a sink, I read the directions and followed
steps 1–10, but at the end, I had not used all the pieces in the box. *Odd,* I
thought. *Maybe they were spares.*

When I turned on the water, it sprayed everywhere in the kitchen.
Frustrated, I decided to hire someone to undo what I had done and

reinstall the faucet correctly. The cost of hiring a plumber was more than double what a regular install would have cost me if I had hired a plumber from the start.

When I recounted the story to my dad, he laughed and made two suggestions. When installing plumbing fixtures, make sure you use all the parts included with the faucet—and hire a plumber. What you might save in the short run will cost more overall. This became another important business mind-set.

How many times do we think that our skill set is "good enough" to handle a problem, task, or installation only to find that our skills fall short of what is needed? Sometimes this realization happens midway through the project. The wise person stops there and gets help. I have been a slow learner and unfortunately would try to power through to the end—only to make matters worse, costlier, and more frustrating.

There is no fault in admitting a lack of knowledge or experience in approaching a situation. There is fault if you approach it without recognizing the pitfalls or the need for experienced advice.

Leave behind and take away: Bravado isn't expertise. Invest in experienced advice to avoid making a mistake that costs more to fix because of inexperience.

Business Mind-Set #25

Envision Success

There is no substitute for hard work. Never give up.
Never stop believing. Never stop fighting.

Hope Hicks

In the summer between my junior and senior years of college, I was accepted into an internship program in Washington, DC. At nineteen, I packed up my car with the clothes I would need and drove to Washington from Cleveland. After six hours of driving, I unpacked my car and went to find something to eat.

On the way back to the apartments where all the interns were staying, I noticed how many parents and family members were helping them move in. The parents fussed and helped their interns, hugged and kissed them, wished them luck in the summer program, and reminded them to be safe.

I was struck by how I had never considered that I would need my parents to help me drive, move in, and get acclimated to Washington. I was so vested in the process that the result consumed my actions and thoughts. It never entered my mind that I couldn't embark on my internship on my own.

It's not that my parents weren't supportive or wouldn't have helped me move in. They supported my participation in the program and visited me in DC. If I had asked, I am sure they would have helped with the driving and moving in. However, I had developed a mind-set of envisioning success with such tunnel vision that if the result could be accomplished on my own, I did so automatically.

This mind-set of seeing our own success tends to translate into consistent daily efforts to turn the vision into reality. Small deposits made in oneself build trust. Making decisions and seeing results will help you achieve your goals.

Leading a company or being an entrepreneur starts with trust in oneself. You will move forward even if the path does not go as planned, events cause you to rethink your vision, lose faith in the agenda, or you have doubts.

Even if you slow down, you won't stop, because you believe in yourself. You believe your vision will succeed because of the deposits you put into your bank account of trust.

I see myself as successful. I hold this belief up to the world's mirror, believe in my vision, and know my vision will end up with the tangible results of success.

Leave behind and take away: Let go of doubts. Believe in your dreams. Believe in yourself.

You can never substitute passion with hard work, but you can use hard work to succeed with your passion.

Reneé Marie Smith, Esq.

About the Author

Renee Marie Smith, Esq. is a nationally recognized entrepreneur, attorney, author, and speaker. A real estate and corporate law specialist, her advice has been featured in Forbes, Huffington Post, and MortgageOrb. As founder of Trending50, an L.A.-based production company for female-centric content, her mission is to educate tomorrow's entrepreneurs today. She also hosts FiF-TV's weekly series "50 Entrepreneurial Women in America." Visit the website at http://www.trending50.com/.